Living in a World of

green

Where Survival Means Blending In

Tanya Lee Stone

BLACKBIRCH PRESS, INC.
WOODBRIDGE, CONNECTICUT

For my mother-in-law Barbara,
with her eyes of green

Published by Blackbirch Press, Inc.
260 Amity Road
Woodbridge, CT 06525

Email: staff@blackbirch.com
Web site: www.blackbirch.com

©2001 by Blackbirch Press, Inc.
First Edition

Printed in the United States

Photo Credits: All images ©Corel Corporation, except
pages 3 (snake), 21: ©PhotoSpin, Inc.; pages 6, 13, 17:
©www.arttoday.com.

10 9 8 7 6 5 4 3 2 1

Library of Congress Cataloging-in-Publication Data
Stone, Tanya Lee.
Living in a world of green / by Tanya Lee Stone.
    p. cm. —
Summary: Introduces ten animals that rely on their
green camouflage to survive in the forest or jungle.
ISBN 1-56711-583-7 (hardcover: alk. paper)
1. Forest animals—Juvenile literature. 2. Camouflage
(Biology)—Juvenile literature[1. Forest animals. 2. Jungle
animals. 3. Camouflage (Biology). 4. Animals.]   I. Title.
QL112.S73 C574 2001
591.47'2—dc21   2001002672

Contents

What do all of the animals in this book have in common?
They all live in a world of green. They make their homes in forests and jungles.
The ten animals in this book are perfectly suited to their environment.
And each relies on camouflage to survive. When something is camouflaged,
it blends into its surroundings and is difficult to see. Camouflage helps these
animals get food and escape danger. How do they do it?

Did You Know?

When a leaf insect is in danger, it will play dead. It can stay completely still for hours until it is sure an enemy is gone.

4

Leaf Insects
Leaf Me Alone!

Look closely at this picture. Is a leaf the only thing you see? A leaf insect seems to disappear while sitting in full view. It has a flat, leaf-shaped body with a large stomach and legs. Its wings are also leaf-shaped. The wings often have lines that look like the veins of a leaf. This type of camouflage is called mimicry. The creature mimics another object to look just like it.

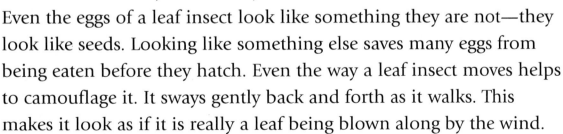

Even the eggs of a leaf insect look like something they are not—they look like seeds. Looking like something else saves many eggs from being eaten before they hatch. Even the way a leaf insect moves helps to camouflage it. It sways gently back and forth as it walks. This makes it look as if it is really a leaf being blown along by the wind.

Did You Know?

- The green treefrog has large, sticky toe pads that help it cling to plants. It also has long legs for jumping—It can leap up to 10 feet (3 meters)!

- The famous Muppet, Kermit the Frog, is a green treefrog.

Tree Frogs

Shades of Green

The green treefrog is an amphibian (an animal that lives both on land and in the water). This treefrog loves forested areas near ponds, lakes, rivers, or marshes. Its beautiful color helps it blend in well in its damp, green environment. The green treefrog can also change color when it needs to. If it is a bright sunny day, the frog's color fades a bit. This helps it absorb less heat and stay cooler. If it is a cloudy day, the frog can darken to soak up more light and heat. It can even fade to a grayish color during the winter to blend in with the duller colors of that season.

Did You Know?

- One stinkbug helps potato farmers protect their crops. Farmers unleash spined soldier bugs to gobble up beetles that can destroy potato fields.

- People in India, Africa, and Mexico eat certain kinds of stinkbugs.

Stinkbugs
What Is That Yucky Smell?!

There are thousands of different kinds of stinkbugs. Like many animals, they are camouflaged by their color and shape. Stinkbugs are usually brown or green to blend in with their surroundings. There are even black stinkbugs that live on dark berry bushes. A stinkbug has a wide, flat body that looks like a shield. Together, its shape and color make it hard to see on leaves and trees. But stinkbugs have an extra weapon that is important in their battle to survive. They stink! When danger is near, a stinkbug lets out a disgusting odor that sends enemies away. This terrible smell often sticks to the leaves the bug was on. The smell keeps a feeding area clear of predators (animals that hunt the stinkbug) for a while so the stinkbug can feast.

Did You Know?

- The longest insect in the world is a walkingstick named Pharnacia kirbyi, which lives in Indonesia. It can be up to 12 inches (30 centimeters) long.

- One type of walkingstick is green and stands upright in the ground to blend in with the grass!

Walkingsticks

Stick Around

Have you ever seen a stick on the ground begin to move? If you have, that was no stick—it was an insect called a walkingstick. Walkingsticks are related to leaf insects. Like leaf insects, walkingsticks can play dead or shed a leg when under attack. Walkingsticks have long, slender bodies with six legs. Their shape and color mimics the look of twigs and sticks. These wingless insects are so well adapted for hiding that they even change color when the leaves and branches do. They are brown in the fall and winter and green in the spring and summer. Their excellent camouflage protects walkingsticks from predators such as lizards, birds, mice, snakes, and frogs. Walkingsticks are so well camouflaged that a bird could land on the same branch and fly away without ever noticing it had been so close to its next meal.

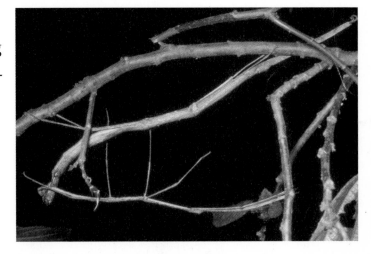

Did You Know?

Swallowtail caterpillars are named for the back wings they grow as butterflies. The wings have stems that look like the sharp tail feathers of the swallow bird.

Swallowtail Caterpillars

Tricky Spots and Smelly Shots

Caterpillars need to eat a lot of leaves before they change into butterflies. But these baby insects have soft bodies and move very slowly. This makes them an easy target for animals that hunt caterpillars for food. Swallowtail caterpillars have adapted clever ways to escape danger. The giant swallowtail uses mimicry to hide in full view. And you won't believe what its brown, white, and black body looks like to other animals—splotches of bird poop! Tiger swallowtails have markings on their backs called eyespots. These large spots look like the eyes of a much bigger animal. This can scare off a predator.

Swallowtail butterfly

Did You Know?

One of the smallest reptiles on Earth is a chameleon. The Pygmy chameleon is less than 2 inches (5 centimeters) long.

14

Chameleons

Quick-Change Artists

Chameleons have an amazing ability to change color quickly. But they don't do it to blend into the background. Their color changes are triggered by heat, light, and the animal's response to an enemy or mate. In fact, a scared chameleon can display dazzling shades of yellow and orange that wouldn't blend into any forest environment! When they are calm, chameleons are a mottled brown or lush green that seems to disappear against the backdrop of the forest. Their thin shape also makes them hard to see in trees.

A chameleon can't hunt or escape quickly, but it doesn't need to. Its feet are designed for grabbing and have sharp claws to dig into tree bark. And each eye moves on its own, so it can see in two different directions without moving its body. A chameleon will sit and wait for a juicy insect meal to pass nearby. Then, in the blink of an eye, it shoots out a long, sticky tongue, zaps its prey, then curls the insect into its mouth.

Butterflies
Flight and Fright

Butterflies are easy prey for birds, wasps, lizards, and spiders. One of the best ways they avoid danger is to fly away. But some butterflies can't fly very fast. And none can outfly a bird. Butterflies use some of the same camouflage defenses as caterpillars. Some have eyespots that frighten predators away. Others have markings that mimic poisonous or bitter-tasting butterflies. This camouflage helps keep the non-poisonous butterflies safe. And lots of butterflies have coloring that blends into the surroundings. They can be drably colored and hard to tell apart from tree branches or bark.

Did You Know?

A sloth only climbs down from its tree once a week to poop. It can take up to an hour for the sloth to reach the ground!

Sloths

Hangin' Around

What spends its whole life hanging upside down in a tree? A sloth. Sloths live in rainforests. They hardly move at all. To eat, they slowly reach out and grab nearby leaves and buds. A sloth has sharp claws and will fight an enemy if attacked. But an animal that moves so slowly can't run away from predators, such as jaguars, snakes, and large birds. It needs a different way to stay out of danger. A sloth's natural gray-brown color blends in well with the forest. This camouflage gets an extra boost from greenish algae that grow in a sloth's fur. A sloth sleeps during the day with its head curled up between its front legs. Together, a sloth's coloring, its sleeping position, and the fact that it barely moves, makes a sloth looks like a stumpy tree branch or a bird nest to predators.

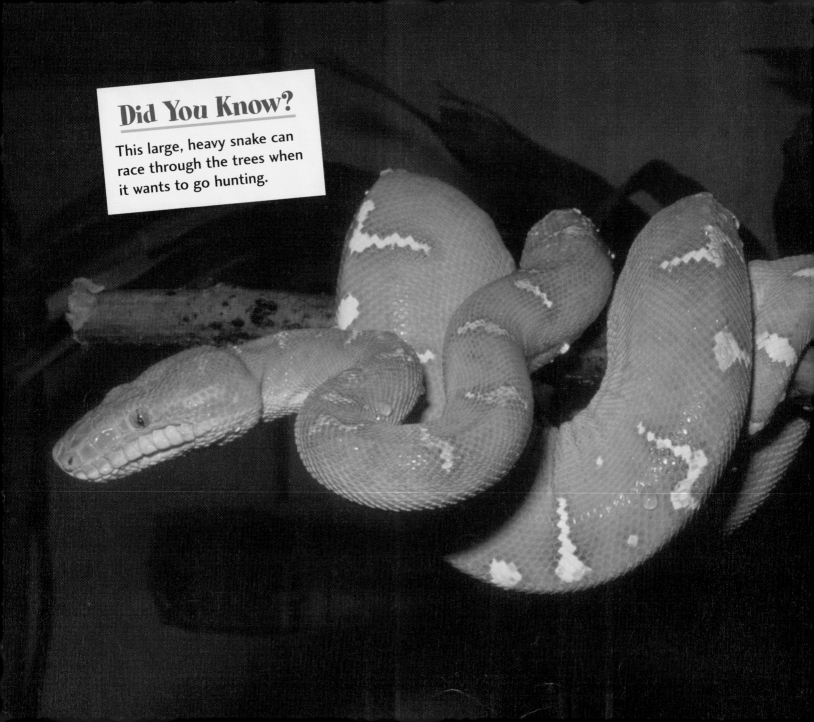

Did You Know?

This large, heavy snake can race through the trees when it wants to go hunting.

Emerald Tree Boas

Sneaky Snakes

The emerald tree boa is a top-notch hunter. But it doesn't usually go searching for prey. Instead, it curls around a tree branch and waits. Camouflage helps this snake stay hidden so it can make a surprise attack when a lizard, bird, or small mammal is nearby. The beautiful green color of the emerald boa blends in well with the rich green colors of the rainforest. It also has white markings to help camouflage it. These markings break up the snake's body shape, making it even harder to see. The white can also look like sunlight streaming through the forest.

Did You Know?

Katydids are named for the song the males sing. It sounds like someone singing "ka-ty-did, ka-ty-didn't!"

Katydids

Hopping Along, Singing a Song

There are thousands of different katydids in forests all over the world. In the Amazon rainforest alone, there are more than 2,000 katydid species. These insects are on the menu for birds, snakes, bats, monkeys, and many other animals. To survive, katydids must be camouflage experts. Many are green and leaf-shaped, which makes them hard to see when they are perched on a plant. Some look like dead, tattered leaves that have fallen to the forest floor. Some even look like tree bark or moss. Others use mimicry so predators will mistake them for stinging insects, such as wasps. Still others change color when the seasons change. Katydids can also escape being eaten by leaping away with their long, powerful back legs.

GLOSSARY

Amphibian A cold-blooded animal that lives both on land and in the water.

Camouflage Any behavior or appearance that helps disguise an animal in its environment.

Insect An animal with three separate body parts—a head, thorax (chest), and abdomen (stomach).

Predator An animal that hunts other animals for food.

Prey An animal that is hunted by another animal.

Mimicry When an animal copies the behavior, smell, or appearance of another animal.

Reptile A cold-blooded animal that lays eggs; a lizard is a type of reptile.

FOR MORE INFORMATION

Books

Gamlin, Linda. *Eyewitness: Evolution*. New York, NY: DK Publishing, 2000.

Legg, Gerald, Carolyn Scrace.. *From Tadpole to Frog*. Danbury, CT: Franklin Watts, 1998.

Wilsdon, Christine. *Insects: National Audubon Society First Field Guides*. New York, NY: Scholastic Trade: 1999.

Web Site

Learn more about jungle animals at: *http://animal.discovery.com/exp/bolivia/bolivia.html*

INDEX